YOU KNOW YOU'RE A CHILD OF THE 1990s WHEN...

Charlie Ellis

summersdale

YOU KNOW YOU'RE A CHILD OF THE 1990s WHEN...

First published in 2011
This revised and updated edition copyright © Summersdale Publishers Ltd, 2016

Illustrations by Rita Kovács; icons © Shutterstock

Summersdale Publishers Ltd
46 West Street
Chichester
West Sussex
PO19 1RP
UK

www.summersdale.com

Printed and bound in China

ISBN: 978-1-84953-896-1

Substantial discounts on bulk quantities of Summersdale books are available to corporations, professional associations and other organisations. For details contact Nicky Douglas by telephone: +44 (0) 1243 756902, fax: +44 (0) 1243 786300 or email: nicky@summersdale.com.

To..

From..

YOU KNOW YOU'RE A CHILD OF THE 1990s WHEN...

You still talk about 'videos', even though you only have DVDs now, and you still 'video' programmes on your TV set-top box.

You used to wear **stick-on** earrings and **transfer tattoos.**

You never could get to grips with those **Magic Eye** pictures but you never let on.

You thought **Hypercolor T-shirts** were the best thing ever invented.

Mr Frosty Ice Maker

Every day was a party when you had a Mr Frosty Ice Maker! The lolly moulds were cool and the ice cubes were fun but everyone knows it's ALL about the slushie maker, situated in Mr Frosty's own belly. Who knew cranking a handle to crush ice could be so much fun!

Furbies

For children, a super-cute furry friend that would talk and play games with you; for adults, the most annoying toy ever invented. This fountain of semi-comprehensible baby talk and painfully audible mechanics was the curse of many households and also responsible for many a battery drought – usually when you had almost taught your Furby to sing.

GAME BOYS

The ultimate status symbol, we begged, pleaded and even did extra chores to get a Game Boy. Although video-game graphics are increasingly 'realistic', we could hold entire worlds in our hands, and experience epic adventures out of just a few little black pixels and a gravelly, but endlessly inventive, 4-bit soundtrack. It also gave your lungs a workout, when the game cartridge needed blowing clean.

YOU KNOW YOU'RE A CHILD OF THE 1990s WHEN...

You feel intensely grateful that Facebook and mobile phones with video recorders didn't exist while you were **learning how to party.**

You used to **call** your friends
at **home,** one by one, to arrange
a time and a place for meeting
them — and you actually turned
up at that place and time.

You used to go shopping for music
in **Our Price** (and possibly pick up
a CD single from **Woolworths**).

Your idea of dancing was lurching
about in a **long jumper** while
looking longingly at the floor.

QUIZ

ONLY A CHILD OF THE 1990s WILL KNOW...

 What food did Badger (of *Bodger and Badger* fame) love?

 Which *Blue Peter* presenter caused scandal when he got sacked?

 What was the name of the spiky-haired, big-bead-wearing rollerblader in *Heartbreak High*?

 What type of animal was Arthur's best friend, Buster?

5 What were the names of the twins from *Rugrats*?

6 Peggy Patch was a character on which show?

7 What was the name Tim's neighbour (whose full face was rarely seen) in *Home Improvement*?

8 Who was the oldest sibling in *My Parents Are Aliens*?

YOU KNOW YOU'RE A CHILD OF THE 1990s WHEN...

You can get a guaranteed laugh
from your friends by saying
'Eranu' in a silly voice or offering
a cup of tea with the words
'Go on, go on, go on, go on...'
in your best Irish accent.

You still secretly believe that 'the truth is out there'.

You're still getting to grips with Damien Hirst's seminal piece *The Physical Impossibility of Death in the Mind of Someone Living,* and it's the reason you've been having nightmares about sharks ever since.

You were impressed by Ally McBeal – not by her high-flying career but because of her **enormous pout**.

DO YOU REMEMBER...

Round the Twist

Was it a fever dream or a real TV show? Either way, it was the trippiest, freakiest, *best* thing on TV and with the catchiest theme song. 'Have you ever...'

The Demon Headmaster

Wait, did we say that *Round the Twist* was the freakiest thing on TV? Actually, it was *The Demon Headmaster*, the show that confirmed our greatest fear: teachers were evil and out to get us. Somehow we managed to ignore the show's other message, though — that computer games were bad for our health.

The Queen's Nose

Annoying sisters, parents not allowing any pets, magic 50p pieces — we all had so much in common with Harmony from *The Queen's Nose*. Well, maybe not the magic coins, although we were sure to give our 50p a little rub, just in case.

Bernard's Watch

It is a truth universally acknowledged that giving Bernard a magic watch was the biggest waste of time ever. He never did anything cool with it! That didn't stop us from spending hours fantasising about what we could achieve if we had a magic watch.

Aquila

If you missed the boat when *Flight of the Navigator* was at the cinema, the short-lived and very British TV series *Aquila* was some consolation. It was about two boys who happen upon a mysterious spaceship – a dream shared by many kids in this UFO-obsessed decade!

ChuckleVision

To me! To you! To me! To you! How many years later and we still can't stop chanting the catchphrase any time we have to carry something in a pair. Barry and Paul were fixtures on the children's TV circuit, although we could never tell which was which.

YOU KNOW YOU'RE A CHILD OF THE 1990s WHEN...

You were the first to imitate **Prodigy** member Maxim (in the video for 'Breathe') by wearing novelty contact lenses – even though the sight of you made small children cry.

You were elated – and endlessly frustrated – with a little game called **Screwball Scramble**.

You wished your parents were Ma and Pop Larkin – then everything would be '**perfick**'!

You spent all of your money in the arcade – on games like *The Simpsons* and *After Burner* – before you even got near the cinema.

QUIZ

ONLY A CHILD OF THE 1990s WILL KNOW...

 1 What year did Jonah Lomu beat the England team in the World Cup, pretty much on his own?

 2 What was UK tennis No. 1 Tim Henman's nickname?

 3 Which part of Evander Holyfield's body did Mike Tyson famously bite?

4 Jimmy Glass scored a last-minute goal, keeping Carlisle in the Football League in 1999. Which position did he play?

5 At the 1992 Barcelona Olympics, which athlete won the men's 100 m gold medal?

6 Gazza cried when England were defeated in the Italia 90 semi-finals by which team?

7 Who helped Derek Redmond over the line in the 1992 Barcelona Olympics men's 400 m semi-final?

8 What was Jean Van de Velde's score on the last hole at the 1999 Open Championship, after his famous 'collapse'?

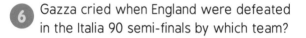

Answers: 1. 1995 **2.** Tiger Tim **3.** His ear **4.** Goalkeeper **5.** Linford Christie **6.** West Germany **7.** His dad **8.** Triple-bogey seven

YOU KNOW YOU'RE A CHILD OF THE 1990s WHEN...

After watching *Four Weddings and a Funeral* when it first came out, you thought all men would be like Hugh Grant – until you started dating.

You always wanted to be
Mr Black in your gang of mates,
but somehow you always
ended up as **Mr Pink**.

You can remember being told off
by your parents for saying 'Eat
my shorts!' to your grandma.

Holidays to **Ibiza**, Magaluf
and **Benidorm** were actually
something to brag about to your
mates (as was the fake gold
jewellery you came back with).

The Simpsons

Who can forget this all-encompassing craze of the 1990s? Matt Groening and Co. made TV history with a show that was as fun for adults as it was for kids. Cue the waves of *Simpsons* merchandise, which included a cassette album entitled *The Simpsons Sing the Blues*, featuring the groovy, epic 'Do the Bartman'.

Friends

Which 'Friend' were you? We got entirely the wrong idea about what it was like to be young and living in New York City, but we loved it anyway. It was pretty much the first box set everyone got and, with ten seasons, there was plenty to be had.

THE FRESH PRINCE OF BEL-AIR

All 1990s children know that the coolest Will Smith character is the Fresh Prince. He had the quickest lines, the most laid-back attitude and the most outrageous clothes. Throw in a brilliant supporting cast – including the ever-goofy Carlton and the dim-witted Jazz – and you have a hit. Here's betting you can rap along to the theme tune!

YOU KNOW YOU'RE A CHILD OF THE 1990s WHEN...

You quizzed the careers officer at school about the qualifications required to be a pet detective after watching *Ace Ventura*.

You feel a certain nostalgia for obvious shop names like **Sock Shop**, Tie Rack and The Sweater Shop – where did they all go?

You went crazy for gross-out toys involving **slime**, gak and **goo**.

You can remember being proud to wear your free **neon** (pink, green or yellow) McDonald's shades that came with your **Happy Meal**.

QUIZ

ONLY A CHILD OF THE 1990s WILL KNOW...

 With what toy could you 'walk the dog' and 'rock the cradle'?

 What rival brand (free in your bag of crisps) competed with Pogs for playground popularity?

 What did the colour black generally indicate on a mood ring?

 What was the last piece to be built in the game Mousetrap?

5 How do you unlock the 'jinx' penalty of silence?

6 What was the name of the original lobster Beanie Baby?

7 What was the name of the elasticated, shirtless doll that also had a bendable canine pal?

8 What was the name of the frustrating memory game you had to 'twist' and 'pull'?

YOU KNOW YOU'RE A CHILD OF THE 1990s WHEN...

You can remember begging your parents for a pair of **Spice Girls**-style chunky-heeled shoes or **Reebok Pumps**. But instead you got something out of the local 'cheap shop'.

You were an **outcast** for
months at school after your
mum wouldn't let you go
grunge on non-uniform day.

You still check under the bed for
Gremlins before going to sleep.

You still have a thing for
Pierce Brosnan – even though
you have to admit that his
Bond was a bit naff.

Titanic

Oh come on, you know you cried while watching *Titanic*. It starts out with heart-throb of the decade Leo being cool and having epic curtains – and then BAM! You're sobbing your heart out with a frosty Kate Winslet. There was totally still room on that raft though...

Jurassic Park

Nothing could prepare us for the terrifying, the thrilling, the dino-riffic *Jurassic Park*. We'd never seen anything like it and we were pretty sure that the dinosaurs were real 'cos there's no way you could fake animals that looked that genuine.

Terminator 2: Judgment Day

Wait – what? The baddie is now... a goodie? Spoilers if you haven't seen *Terminator 2* yet but c'mon! If you haven't then you've deprived yourself of one of the coolest films ever! (Although if you had seen the first film before T2 came out, your parents were obviously way cool.)

The Lion King

Some people like to waffle about how the film is based on *Hamlet* but, frankly, who cares? There are singing lions, singing hyenas, and singing *and* farting warthogs. The 1990s was a classic era for blockbusting Disney films – and this is arguably the best.

Four Weddings and a Funeral

At the time, it wasn't clear what this film was about. You only knew two things about it: your mum would watch it on VHS and cry – but it was still her favourite movie – and it was one of the umpteen-billion films featuring Hugh Grant and his floppy hair.

Home Alone

For several blissful days, Kevin McCallister lived the life we dreamed about (except for the part about being terrorised by burglars): eating whatever he wanted, watching whatever he wanted, no one to boss him around... And we may have tried to make an ill-advised booby trap or two ourselves.

YOU KNOW YOU'RE A CHILD OF THE 1990s WHEN...

You desperately wanted to pass your driving test so that you and your mates could re-enact the 'Bohemian Rhapsody' head-banging scene in *Wayne's World*.

You still haven't lived down the time when your mates convinced you to ask the lady at the Boots counter for some *Fight Club* soap.

Your parents let you redecorate your bedroom after being inspired by *Changing Rooms* – and it ended up looking like a tart's boudoir, of course.

You remember having your first email account and being really excited about getting messages – even the ones that just said 'Message Undeliverable'.

QUIZ

ONLY A CHILD OF THE 1990s WILL KNOW...

 What was the name of Biff, Chip and Kipper's dog?

 Which 1990s classic opens with 'On a dark, dark hill there was a dark, dark town'?

 Name at least two of the original Animorphs.

 Complete this title: *Diary of a __ Cat*.

5 The care home that Tracy Beaker lived in was nicknamed what?

6 How many strawberries does the very hungry caterpillar eat?

7 With what vehicle did Harry and Ron arrive at Hogwarts at the start of *Harry Potter and the Chamber of Secrets*?

8 How did the Jolly Postman deliver his letters?

YOU KNOW YOU'RE A CHILD OF THE 1990s WHEN...

You can't think of a single Shakespeare play without an image of **Kenneth Branagh** popping into your head.

You couldn't wait for
Ant and Dec to break into the
PokéRap on *SM:TV*.

You would gladly eat
Findus Crispy Pancakes.

You wouldn't consider going
out without squirting yourself
all over with **CK One.**

Scrunchies

If your scrunchy wasn't bigger than your head then you just weren't cool. Not really, but it was true that the bigger the scrunchie, the better. A scrunchie matched to your top was a fashion must.

Choker Necklaces

Any choker was great but the best of all were those 'tattoo' stretch ones. You could get them at any good Claire's Accessories and even in those one-pound machines. Paired with a handful of other pendant necklaces to look your best.

JELLY
SANDALS

What's better than jelly sandals? Glitter jelly sandals! Uncomfortable, strappy and a bit sticky, the jelly sandal was nonetheless the most beloved item in our wardrobe. Wearing those made you feel like a modern, funky princess.

YOU KNOW YOU'RE A CHILD OF THE 1990s WHEN...

You remember what you were doing the moment you heard that **Take That** had split up (or, if you weren't so boy-band-inclined, the day you found out that **Kurt Cobain** had died).

You only agreed to go on a **date** with the boy next door because he had tickets to see **Oasis**.

You once owned a whole set of **neon-coloured socks**.

You still have the nickname 'Streaky' due to the badly applied **fake tan** you used to slap on before school.

QUIZ

ONLY A CHILD OF THE 1990s WILL KNOW...

 What was the name of the tiny crunchy candy that came in a box of two halves, with two different flavours?

2 What Right Said Fred song did Fruitella adapt for a famous 1990s advert?

 There was a classic lunchtime ham that came in two colours: which animal's head were they in the shape of?

4 What flavour was Scary Spice's lollipop in the Spice Girls' branded lolly collection?

5 Finish this famous food advertisement catchphrase: 'I feel like — tonight'.

6 What was the name of the unusual 'clear cola' that appeared in shops in the early 1990s? (Clue: it's also a key on a computer keyboard.)

7 What were the two initial variations of Sunny D, named after US states?

8 What was the name of the Weetos mascot?

YOU KNOW YOU'RE A CHILD OF THE 1990s WHEN...

You remember the **pain of** having to wait until your video (or album cassette) **rewound.** It felt like an eternity!

You went around to a friend's house mostly because they had a **SodaStream.**

You have fond memories of singing: '**Gillette,** the best a man can get!' to your brother after he incurred his first shaving injury.

You have an irresistible urge to shout '**Nicole!**' when you see a woman driving a **Renault Clio,** and '**Papa!**' when it's a man.

Crew-neck Jumpers

These jumpers weren't for wearing; they were for tying around your waist. And also for inevitably getting caught in the chain when you tried to cycle with them on.

Baseball Caps

It's said that scientists have studied for years to discover the exact coolest angle to wear a baseball cap. They're still not sure but it seems to be at any angle but facing the front.

Polo Necks

Now we think of it, it's not clear why the jumper beloved of librarians and embarrassing dads everywhere was so in, but it was. And we have the photos, sadly, to prove it.

Puka Shell Necklaces

We may not have ever seen a surfboard in our lives, let alone Hawaii, but puka shell necklaces were a must-have item. Strangely, jewellery for dudes hasn't really been in fashion since. Wonder why...

Baggy

So 'baggy' isn't really an item of clothing or jewellery, but for us 1990s kids, it was a way of life. Whether you were grunge or loved rap, the name of the game was baggy jeans, topped by a baggy tee, topped by a baggy shirt, topped by a baggy sweatshirt.

YOU KNOW YOU'RE A CHILD OF THE 1990s WHEN...

You're still wondering why **Madonna** named her daughter after a cricket ground.

You remember the first time you saw *The Jerry Springer Show* – and it blew your mind!

You borrowed your dad's **Handycam** to make your own version of *The Blair Witch Project*.

You laughed your head off when someone told you we'd **win the Ashes** in Australia one day.

QUIZ

ONLY A CHILD OF THE 1990s WILL KNOW...

 Which of these were NOT a 1990s celebrity couple?
   A. Brad and Angelina
   B. Johnny and Winona
   C. Britney and Justin

 Who was the highest-paid actor in Hollywood in 1995? (Clue: he starred in *Judge Dredd* in that year.)

 Frances Bean Cobain was born in which year?

4 Which famous woman starred alongside Michael Jackson in the video for his 1995 song 'You Are Not Alone?

5 Liz Hurley wore a black dress famously held together by what?

6 Stephen Gately came out as gay in 1999; he was a member of which boy band?

7 Madonna's iconic cone bra was designed by which fashion designer?

8 Orange soda was the favourite drink of which kids' sit-com character?

YOU KNOW YOU'RE A CHILD OF THE 1990s WHEN...

The words **'Gareth Southgate'**
and **'penalties'** still make
you angry.

You remember **Harry Potter** best as a character in a book — not as a child movie star.

You always get the irresistible urge to re-enact the iconic prow scene in *Titanic* whenever you find yourself on a **ferry**.

You still believe, in all honesty, that you are **Bridget Jones** (or Mark Darcy).

Curtains

Sigh. This floppy, gelled 'do was the province of heart-throbs everywhere, from David Beckham to Leonardo DiCaprio. The only way for a hairstyle to be more 1990s was if you added highlights.

Tiny Buns

With one of the decade's more... original styles, girls everywhere wondered: why have one bun on your head when you could have a dozen? Fixed in place with miniscule, painful rubber bands, the effect was 'nobbly', to say the least.

THE RACHEL

No list of 1990s hairstyles can go without mention of The Rachel. Highlights, layers, *Friends*; it was like someone took the decade and made it into a haircut. To our disappointment, getting The Rachel didn't make us look like Jennifer Anniston, though.

YOU KNOW YOU'RE A CHILD OF THE 1990s WHEN...

You remember having heated
'Oasis vs Blur'
debates with your friends.

You indulged in the see-through, **coloured plastic dummy** craze while at school.

You thought having a **pager** was the height of modern technological advancement.

Mario Kart, *Street Fighter II* and *Doom* were (and still are) at the top of your **Super Nintendo** video game favourites list.

QUIZ

ONLY A CHILD OF THE 1990s WILL KNOW...

 What was the highest-selling video game of the 1990s? (Clue: it was for Game Boy)

 Who starred as the Gamesmaster on the hit show of the same name?

 What species is Mario's nemesis Bowser?

 The DualShock controller enhanced gameplay in what way?

5 What technological innovation made running, or even walking, with Discmans much easier?

6 Before mobile phones were widespread, what text-only gadget was used for high-speed communication in the 1990s?

7 Which Apple product, famous for its jazzy casing, brought the company back into profitability?

8 The Dreamcast console, now defunct, was released by which company in 1998?

YOU KNOW YOU'RE A CHILD OF THE 1990s WHEN...

You begged your parents to buy you the new – bigger, badder – **Super Soaker** after seeing the ad on TV.

Bill and Ted, Beavis and Butt-Head, and **Thelma and Louise** are some of your on-screen heroes.

You have fond memories of the phrases **'Gladiators, rrready?'**, 'Tooo the Crystal Dome!' and 'It's good, but it's not right.'

Kickers moccasins were as cool as it got.

DO YOU REMEMBER...

'Wannabe'

It didn't matter what music you were into, by the end of 1996 you knew all the words to this song. Kicking off the brief world-domination of the Spice Girls and 'girl power', kids everywhere blasted this from their tape players.

'Spaceman'

To be honest, the best bit of this song by Babylon Zoo was the first 30 seconds, but what a good start it was! We were getting ever-closer to the millennium and this tune sounded like the future was arriving.

'Bittersweet Symphony'

If you're going to have a massive hit, it's probably best to release 'Bittersweet Symphony' – the song that was *everywhere*. You will probably recall The Verve's epic people-barging video, which you would have watched on *Top of the Pops* (or, if you were lucky enough, MTV or The Box).

'Smells Like Teen Spirit'

Either someone took all your angst and made it into a perfect song or you were listening to a wall of senseless noise; Nirvana's 'Teen Spirit' wasn't for everyone, but for those who appreciated it, it was the start of a love affair with grunge.

'Parklife'

So Blur were in a fight with Oasis and this is a song about pigeons and parks? We weren't too clear on the details at the time but we knew one thing: this is a tune!

'... Baby One More Time'

Strangely sad lyrics? Check. Inappropriate schoolgirl uniform? Big check. And yet somehow this was a pop smash hit, transforming Britney Spears into a super-megastar!

YOU KNOW YOU'RE A CHILD OF THE 1990s WHEN...

You remember
Arnold Schwarzenegger
better as an A-list movie star,
rather than a laughable politician.

You can remember the
heart-stopping moment when
Neighbours character **Harold**
disappeared!

You still haven't got
used to referring to
Opal Fruits as Starburst.

Even after two decades, you still
can't get your **Tamagotchi** to
survive longer than two weeks.

QUIZ

ONLY A CHILD OF THE 1990s WILL KNOW...

 In the lamentable 1993 film *Super Mario Bros.*, Mario is played by which actor?

 In *Jurassic Park*, the velociraptors are defeated by which dinosaur?

 Who wrote the soundtrack for the 1992 Disney smash hit, *The Lion King*?

 Which famous showstopping song do the Gremlins, in *Gremlins 2: The New Batch*, sing near the end of the film?

5 What was the model number of the terminator chasing John Connor in *Terminator 2*?

6 *Clueless* was an updated film version of which classic novel? (Clue: it's by Jane Austen.)

7 What colour pill did Neo take in order to 'wake up' to reality?

8 In the Austin Powers sequel, *The Spy Who Shagged Me*, what precious item did Austin lose?

YOU KNOW YOU'RE A CHILD OF THE 1990s WHEN...

You know what **Pogs** and **Tazos** are, but never quite figured out how to use them.

You know how to
'party like it's **1999**'.

90210 just doesn't sound the
same without **Beverly Hills**
in front of it.

You were shocked to discover
that *Northern Exposure* wasn't
filmed in Alaska.

'Whassup?'

Whhaaaaaassssuuuuuuuup? No further discussion
needed.

'Take a Chill Pill'

When parents, teachers and friends alike were
all getting lairy and you weren't having it, telling
them to take a chill pill was the obvious solution.
Surprisingly, the advice rarely helped people to
calm down.

'Massive'

Both an adjective and a noun – to be used
respectively to refer to something that was
completely awesome, or to your friends' group
or collective. Big up to the Skegness massive!

'... NOT!'

To be said loudly and with great defiance at the end of a sentence that you didn't mean, this was our first foray into the usually-more-subtle world of sarcasm. Also, one of the many 1990s catchphrases popularised by hard-rockin' duo Wayne and Garth (Mike Myers and Dana Carvey), of *Saturday Night Live*, *Wayne's World* and *Wayne's World 2* fame. Party on!

NOT!

YOU KNOW YOU'RE A CHILD OF THE 1990s WHEN...

A moustache didn't look good
on anyone – except your dad,
Nigel Mansell and **Hulk Hogan**.

You didn't see anything
wrong with spending your
Friday night watching *TFI Friday*
and *The Word*.

If someone mentions **Gazza**, you
immediately think of a kebab.

You thought you sounded
particularly smart when informing
your friends that **Hercule Poirot**
was Belgian, not French.

QUIZ

ONLY A CHILD OF THE 1990s WILL KNOW...

 1 Which transport link between London and Paris was opened in May 1994?

2 Diana, Princess of Wales, received media acclaim when she took her sons to which British theme park in 1993?

3 Before 1992, the Premier League was originally known as what?

 4 What was the name of the world's first successfully cloned mammal?

5 What was the name of the UK's 1997 Eurovision-winning single? (Clue: it was performed by Katrina and the Waves.)

6 In 1994, which sport did basketball god Michael Jordan switch to?

7 The World Wide Web was made public in what year?

8 What was the name of the intern that President Bill Clinton 'did not' have sexual relations with?

YOU KNOW YOU'RE A CHILD OF THE 1990s WHEN...

You have fond memories of reading *Smash Hits*, *FHM*, *Mixmag* and *J-17*.

Going to superclubs like
Gatecrasher, Cream
and **Godskitchen** was
the equivalent of reaching the
Emerald City in *The Wizard of Oz*.

You logically thought:
the **bigger** the speakers,
the **louder** the music.

Batman and Robin means
Del Boy and **Rodney**.

Dial-up

Sometimes, when it's quiet, we can still hear the screeching of a dial-up modem ringing in our ears. Oh the days when you would try to sneak as much time on the internet as possible, while your parents shouted for you to get off because they wanted to use the phone.

The Millennium Bug

It was pretty much the coming of the apocalypse: the millennium bug was going to shut down everything electronic and completely wipe the internet – and we wouldn't even be able to go on AOL. The end was truly nigh.

NOKIA 5110

In the late 1990s, mobile phones were IT –
and, as with everything else, it mattered
what brand of phone you had! Never mind
having the internet or a camera on there, it
was quite enough having a
personalised monophonic
ringtone and *Snake*.

YOU KNOW YOU'RE A CHILD OF THE 1990s WHEN...

You think the sound of **monks singing** doesn't quite work unless there's an **electronic beat** in the background.

You can't get **'I'll be back'**
out of your vocabulary.

You remember a time when
you could take a **penknife** and
a razor in your hand luggage,
and nobody in airport **security**
would bat an eyelid.

You know all the words to
'Don't Look Back in Anger',
but you still don't really know
what the song's about.

QUIZ

ONLY A CHILD OF THE 1990s WILL KNOW...

 Which Carter was a member of the Backstreet Boys?
- A. Nick Carter
- B. Aaron Carter
- C. John Carter

 What was the title of All Saints' debut single? (Clue: 'I Know…')

 Baddiel and Skinner teamed up with which band to re-release their anthem 'Three Lions' in 1998?

4 Which Gallagher brother referred to Robbie Williams as the 'fat dancer from Take That'?

5 Whitney Houston stayed at the UK No.1 slot with 'I Will Always Love You' for how many weeks?

6 Which controversial Prodigy video won Best Dance Video and Breakthrough Video at the 1998 MTV Video Music Awards?

7 What species was the pitiful main character in Daft Punk's 'Da Funk' video?

8 Madonna released a coffee table book in 1992 titled what?

YOU KNOW YOU'RE A CHILD OF THE 1990s WHEN...

You aspired to be like – at least – one of the characters in *Saved by the Bell* (except maybe Screech!).

£2 coins still feel like an innovation, and the 5p, 10p and 50p coins still seem a bit too small.

You remember feeling, in the middle of a spring night in 1997, that 'Things Can Only Get Better'.

You thought **Manchester United**'s title supremacy wouldn't last much longer.

DO YOU REMEMBER...

Sony Walkman/Discman

The 1990s were a time of great revolution for portable music! At the start we were buying all our favourite singles on tape, and by the end of the decade, we were struggling through errantly skipping albums and buying fancy cases for our CD collections. If you wanted to be different (and had the cash), there was also something called MiniDisc.

Super Nintendo

Nintendo had already proven they were kings of video game consoles, with the legendary NES. Like everything in the 1990s, sticking 'super' in front of a name was all it took to make it sound like the best thing ever. The Super Nintendo might have been just that – especially if you got hold of a copy of the highly anticipated *Street Fighter II*.

PlayStation

Crash Bandicoot, Spyro the Dragon, Lara Croft, Abe, Rayman – for years these were our good buddies, transporting us to new worlds. Although, with the highs come the lows: remember the pain of scratching a disc or trying to decide which game to delete off your memory card to make way for your new save?

Floppy Disks

Remember all those films where the hero needed to steal some world-saving information and it was all on a super hi-tech floppy disk? Remember when one of those hi-tech floppy disks would get stuck in your computer and you had to raid the cutlery drawer to get it out? We never saw that in the movies!

Sega Mega Drive

Sonic the Hedgehog, *Streets of Rage*, *Micro Machines*… The 1990s really were the glory days of gaming. The only downside was falling out with our Super Nintendo-owning friends over which console was better.

Easy-Bake Oven

Doing chores was rubbish but having an Easy-Bake Oven was the coolest! A dusty ancestor of the meal-in-a-mug trend, all you had to do was press a button and you'd made some cake – or at least that's what it seemed like. If only we were as keen on cooking now.

YOU KNOW YOU'RE A CHILD OF THE 1990s WHEN...

You remember telling your friends that *The Lord of the Rings* was too huge and epic to ever appear as a film (especially having seen the disjointed 1978 attempt!).

You owned a **zebra-print**
slap bracelet.

You remember when wearing
a **shell suit** was totally
unremarkable – and when
wearing a turquoise shell suit
meant you'd had a **New Age**
religious experience.

Jeremy Beadle was a popular TV
celebrity (except for the people he
pranked in *Beadle's About*).

QUIZ

ONLY A CHILD OF THE 1990s WILL KNOW...

1 Which girly, flight-capable toy was recalled in 2000 after causing more than 100 injuries since its 1994 release?

2 In the board game *Gooey Louie*, what was the main method of play?

3 What miniscule hero was sold with playsets named 'Doom Zones' and 'Horror Heads'?

4 What colour was the electronic voice-recorder Dear Diary?

5 What toy's appeal lay in your ability to draw on it, only to wash it all off and start again?

6 The chunky spring-loaded shoes loved by kids the world over were called:

    A. Gravity Boots

    B. Space Hoppers

    C. Moon Shoes

7 How did you 'heal' the injured Animal Hospital toys?

8 What was the name of the garden playset consisting of a ball attached to a pole and two racquets?

YOU KNOW YOU'RE A CHILD OF THE 1990s WHEN...

You remember when **Big Brother** was just something scary in a George Orwell novel.

You're glad that **giant headphones** are cool again – you can get your old ones out of the attic!

Rollerblades (and to some extent 'quads') were the most street-credible mode of transport.

The 'Macarena' was played at least twice at your school **disco**.

Kate Moss

Was there anything more 1990s than Kate Moss modelling for Calvin Klein? Fresh-faced and waifish, she was the complete opposite of the tall and curvy supermodels of the day, such as Cindy Crawford and fellow Brit Naomi Campbell.

Dave Benson Phillips

Champion of children, gunger of grown-ups, Dave Benson Phillips was our hero! We would sit, wide-eyed, as he orchestrated the gungings of strict parents and overbearing teachers alike.

NOEL EDMONDS AND MR BLOBBY

Children's TV stalwart Noel Edmonds became beloved of a whole new generation with *Noel's House Party*. He soon introduced fan favourite Mr Blobby, which we remember as being hilarious at the time but, looking back, appears to be slightly nightmarish!

YOU KNOW YOU'RE A CHILD OF THE 1990s WHEN...

You developed frostbite in your midriff because of your insistence on wearing **crop tops** in any weather – or got injured from wearing holographic 'Lennon' **sunglasses** at night.

You had a massive crush on **Aladdin** and/or **Jasmine**.

You still can't get over how Batman films went from gothic (*Batman*, ***Batman Returns***) to goofy (*Batman Forever*, ***Batman and Robin***). George Clooney – what were they thinking?!

You tried to tell your parents that you **wouldn't get out of bed** for less than 10,000 sweets a day.

QUIZ

ONLY A CHILD OF THE 1990s WILL KNOW...

 Who asked a surprised Debbie McGee, 'So, what first attracted you to the millionaire Paul Daniels?'

2 What was Victor Meldrew's catchphrase?

3 Matt Lucas rose to fame as George Dawes, who dressed as what?

 What was the catchphrase of lead character Dr Sam Beckett in *Quantum Leap*?

5 Although airing in the 1990s, *Heartbeat* was set in which decade?

6 What was the name of Marshall's best friend and sidekick in *Eerie, Indiana*?

7 Jet, Rhino and Wolf all featured in which television series?

8 *The New Adventures of Superman* featured which actor in the lead role of Clark Kent / Superman?

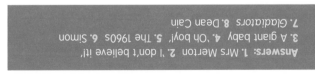

YOU KNOW YOU'RE A CHILD OF THE 1990s WHEN...

You spent the last half of 1999 doing *Matrix* slo-mo bends in the playground.

You owned weekend trainers,
everyday trainers and
'formal' trainers.

You knew all the words to 'Ironic',
even if you didn't exactly know
what 'ironic' meant.

You pretty much melted
your tongue off with a
Warhead sour sweet.

Taz Bars

Taz was one of the main dudes of the decade and his chocolate bar was no exception. Way cooler than his all-chocolate counterpart Freddo, Taz bars not only had caramel centres but were also only 10 p, guaranteeing maximum bang for your pocket-money buck.

Panda Pops

This warm 'strawberry jelly and ice cream'-flavoured fizzy drink was bought at the school canteen or local village hall. Mmmm... delicious! Actually, not really delicious, but affordable on a pocket-money budget.

BIG BABY POPS

We're not really sure why an undersized baby's bottle full of sherbet was so popular, but it was something to do with the cheesy and immensely catchy advert, which reliably informed us we could lick, dip, shake *and* suck the toy. The novelty factor was the main draw, as was the case with similar sweets like Push Pops and Chupa Chups with bubblegum inside.

YOU KNOW YOU'RE A CHILD OF THE 1990s WHEN...

You can still remember the
football chants of your youth:
'Ooh aah Cantona!'

You can remember a time when a can of **cola** was less than 50p.

You went to **John Menzies** or **Woolworths** for all your school stationery needs.

You sort of looked like a bug, with your scraped-back **ponytail** and two strands of hair coming down your face.

QUIZ

ONLY A CHILD OF THE 1990s WILL KNOW...

 The dubious combination of skirt and shorts was known as what?

 Naomi Campbell took a tumble on the runway modelling for which designer? (Clue: V. W.)

 If you crossed a belt and an oversized wallet, what would you get?

 What kind of hairdressing implement has a sprit level?

5 What was the name for the waifish, gaunt style of high fashion?

6 What type of childish dress was beloved of the riot grrl and grunge movements?

7 What body piercing came to popularity after Christy Turlington showed off hers in 1993?

8 What was the name of the leggings with straps that slipped under the heel?

YOU KNOW YOU'RE A CHILD OF THE 1990s WHEN...

At least half your pocket money
was spent on **hair gel.**

You remember a time when the only music you could buy on vinyl was for **dance music** DJs.

You bore witness to the unholy union of two of the decade's most popular **music** genres: rap and metal. And so it was that 'Nu Metal' was created.

You were never worried about where your wallet was because it was in your pocket, attached by your trusty **wallet chain**.

Troll Dolls

The beauty of Troll Dolls was that there were just *so many*. Big ones, small ones, pencil toppers, backpacks – they were everywhere. Our room looked like some sort of sci-fi nightmare.

Alien Birthpods

Speaking of sci-fi nightmares, Alien Birthpods combined two of the 1990s' biggest trends: aliens and goo. The pinnacle of gross-out toys, for some reason digging around in an egg full of goo for two rubbery alien babies was strangely compelling.

Pokémon Cards

The purists will argue that the cards are a mere commercialisation of the games, but who cared – there were 'shinies' to be found and trades to be made. Very little actual gameplay went on; it was far more satisfying to sit and compare whose deck was better than whose.

Football Stickers

When the Euro 1996 football sticker album came out, suddenly everyone in the playground was a hardened negotiator. A Paul Ince for an Alan Shearer? You must be having a laugh.

Skateboards

Remember: those who can't, fingerskate. And actually, apart from the blessed few, those who couldn't still tried to skate. We may have just about been able to mount the kerb but we had dreams of massive half pipes and being christened 'the new Tony Hawk'.

Backpacks

Tiny backpacks, smiley-face backpacks, furry backpacks, animal backpacks – there was seemingly no end to how cool they were. And if your backpack *wasn't* cool, you could tag it so it looked awesome (to the annoyance of the parent who had just bought it).

YOU KNOW YOU'RE A CHILD OF THE 1990s WHEN...

You thought anything could be made out of just a few sheets of tissue paper and three-parts water, one-part **PVA glue**.

You owned a pair of
popper-fastened
tracksuit bottoms.

Your fave bands were all a
strange mix of letters and
numbers: **911, A1, 3T...**

Your parents had to cut out
at least one **twisty hair gem**
from your hair.

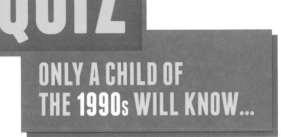

QUIZ

ONLY A CHILD OF THE 1990s WILL KNOW...

 Skechers put themselves on the map with a trainer named what? (Clue: Round, shiny metal.)

 Which popular 1990s brand had a kangaroo logo?

 What was the preferred strap styling for dungarees in the 1990s?

 The windcheater was a popular style of which item of clothing?

5 Which style of jean was created by tumbling the denim in bleach?

6 Which brand of slightly frog-eyed sports sunglasses were a big hit during the decade?

7 Reebok shoes advertised that what body part was going to get you?

8 JNCO jeans were associated with fans of which sport?

YOU KNOW YOU'RE A CHILD OF THE 1990s WHEN...

You aspired to own a mountain
bike with **RockShox**.

The words 'ice-cream-flavoured Chewits' sound appealing.

After seeing it used to such brilliant effect in *Home Alone 2*, the top of your Christmas list was a Talkboy.

Everything was 'phat' (that's with a 'ph').

Sally Gunnell

Actually, that's Sally Gunnel MBE as of 1993 and OBE as of 1998. She was Britain's hero in the 1992 Olympics and then a heartbreaker at the 1996 Olympics when an old injury flared up and she had to pull out of the 400 m women's sprint semi-finals. Oh Sally, we loved you.

Jonah Lomu

If a mad scientist had built a robot with the sole purpose of creating the best rugby player ever, then they surely couldn't have created a more fearsome beast than Jonah Lomu. Long and lanky, he didn't look exactly like the rugby players of the time, but then it was hard to get a good look when he was flying past you to score a try.

EURO 1996

There were highs and there were lows: Germany actually winning the thing in our own backyard was embarrassing, as was Gazza's dye job. But mainly it was totally rad that football had come home.

YOU KNOW YOU'RE A CHILD OF THE 1990s WHEN...

You indicated that things were all cool with a casual 'Cowabunga, dude'.

You thought that **French Bread Pizzas** were one of the best microwave foods ever invented.

You ate unholy amounts of **cereal** just to get more tiny plastic **prizes**... pencil toppers, spoon toppers, anything!

You were captivated by the idea of a **warehouse rave** (but had no clue how to find or get to one).

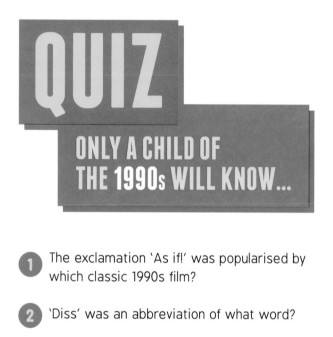

QUIZ

ONLY A CHILD OF THE 1990s WILL KNOW...

1. The exclamation 'As if!' was popularised by which classic 1990s film?

2. 'Diss' was an abbreviation of what word?

3. 'Dumb babies' was the go-to response of which *Rugrats* character?

4. Which Tom Hanks film line was used to annoy joggers and people running to catch a train?

5 If someone isn't that impressive, they are not 'all that and a bag of…' what?

6 Inspired by the advert, what did people recite as they ate their Jaffa Cake?

7 'Fo shizzle my nizzle' was popularised by which American rapper?

8 The 'double loser' hand gesture could combine to create the sign for which other flippant phrase?

Answers: 1. Clueless **2.** Disrespect **3.** Angelica **4.** 'Run, Forrest, Run!' **5.** Chips **6.** Full moon, half moon, total eclipse **7.** Snoop Dogg **8.** 'W' for 'whatever'

123

YOU KNOW YOU'RE A CHILD OF THE 1990s WHEN...

Your dream house is one entirely furnished with **inflatable chairs.**

Your parents used to have to physically pry you out of the **Gadget Shop.**

You had to go to the **DOS** part of your computer to launch **video games.**

You owned *at least* 30 different smelly gel pens.

Goosebumps books

They weren't kidding around when they said you were in for a scare. Never mind all the horror films and violent video games your parents were trying to protect you from – the real nightmares were contained in these books.

Sweet Valley High

Oh those twins, just living normal lives as stunningly beautiful, wealthy teens surrounded by their similarly beautiful and wealthy friends. We couldn't get enough of all the low-stakes drama, make-ups and break-ups that took place at *Sweet Valley High*.

Anne Fine

If Anne Fine had just written *Madame Doubtfire* then she would have been our childhood hero. But no, she whacked out winners like nobody's business: *Flour Babies*, *The Diary of a Killer Cat*, *Charm School*. We might as well have just had a shelf dedicated to her.

The Magic Key

Do you remember learning with Biff, Chip and Floppy the dog? Whoever thought to make learning to read fun by throwing in some magic and time travel had the right idea — we loved it!

Horrible Histories

Often sold as 'history with all the nasty bits left in', we spent hours poring over queen-killing Tudors and suffering medieval peasants, leaving us strangely knowledgeable about very specific, very bloody, parts of history.

Jacqueline Wilson

Funny, moving and sometimes a little naughty, Jacqueline Wilson's stories are highly relatable. Her heroines were brave and had strong personalities, and while their situations were often very sad, you knew that Ms Wilson would help them find happiness in the end. Plus those amazing illustrations by Nick Sharratt!

If you're interested in finding out more about our books, find us on Facebook at **Summersdale Publishers** and follow us on Twitter at **@Summersdale**.

www.summersdale.com